TRUST THE CEREMONY, F*CK THE CEREMONY, TRUST THE CEREMONY

Poems

Ryan Van Lenning

Copyright © 2025
by Wild Nature Heart Press

All rights reserved.
Use of this material with attribution is welcome.

For inquires, contact
ryan@wildnatureheart.com

Cover Design by author

ISBN: 978-1-7368776-2-3

WildNatureHeart.com

Other Books By the Author

In the Re-Membering Series:

Re-Membering
One Bright and Real Caress
From Inside These Wild Ones

Forthcoming:
Becoming Beautiful Barbarians
An Ambitious Silence
Riverever

*For Larry Hobbs
and his Whale Ears of Deep Listening*

For all my guides

*For all those who cross the threshold
into Ceremony*

CONTENTS

INTRODUCTION 1
TRUST THE CEREMONY 10
   Arrive 11
   Desert Doorway 13
   Walk Away, Invisible One 15
   Door-To-Mystery-Knows-Where 17
   Tender Beauty of the Breakdown 18
   Desert Vows 20
   A Dis-/Per-/Con-Cussion 22
   Let the Mountain Carve You 24
   Species of Surrender 26
   Make a Ceremony of It 28
   Dust On Her Feet 30
   No Lies On the Mountain 31
   It Just Is 32
   Stone Buddies 34
   This Breath 36
   Knock and See What Answers 38
FUCK THE CEREMONY 39
   Juniper Dreams and Piñon Nightmares 40
   Sidewinding Ceremony 42
   Wound and Not the Story of the Wound 43
   The Shape of Death, The Shape of Life 46
   The Sky Is Blue 49
   At the Feet of That Brutal, Beloved Teacher 52
   Each Inch Etches Something Holy 54
   Stoned 57
   So, Crack 60

When It Booms From Below 63
A Ripe and Relentless Cracking 65
Caterpillar Dreams 67
TRUST THE CEREMONY 69
Within Your Wings of Trickster Trusts 70
Guttural Utterance of Holy Unknowing 71
We Dream the Butterfly 72
That Tide Your Heartbeat 74
If Today Is Not the Day 76
Trust, Beaver 77
Wild Syllable of Trust on Your Lips 78
Next Time She Draws Blood 79
Circulation 81
Serviceable Conduit 83
Keep Walking, Visible One 84
Always Here 85
Spiraling Up (Cairns of Holy Longing) 87
The Experiment Isn't Over 92
The Path Is Made 94
On the North Face It 95
Cupcake Buffaloes 97
The Ceremony Is Messy and Perfect 100
Epilogue 102
Does a Little Speck Remain? 103
About the Author 105
About Wild Nature Heart 106
Titles in the *Re-Membering* Series 107
Excerpts From Upcoming Books 111

INTRODUCTION

To Begin

The trailhead is such a magnificent moment, carrying its own species of energy. It is a threshold of sorts—the threshold into the unknown. Whether that is an actual trail, a new adventure, endeavor, diagnosis, experiment, or connection, or a stepping over the threshold in wilderness ceremony—it is a crossing from one world to another.

An excitement and curiosity can run the blood hot regardless of the weather. What beauties and mysteries does the land hold? How will this re-wild me, return me? What aspects of Life will the journey help me re-member, reclaim?

The threshold also marks our trepidations, surfaces our fears, for we know we will be changed by the journey—we will return a different person. With new scratches and bruises, yes, but also perhaps new gifts, new perspectives.

The journey may likely stretch us into a different shape.

Oh what fantastic trust that requires! It's a beautiful–sometimes naive, always remarkable–trust that subsidizes stepping out onto a path.

Truth be told, it is a risk to set off into the unknown. Am I up for climbing this mountain? For completing this new project? For entangling with this new person? Un-entangling from an old weave? To let the world see *this* part of me?

Can I absorb this Mystery? Is my body capable? Is my psyche rooted? Am I prepared? What about my old life, habits, patterns—which of those will the journey/ceremony/mountain/trail threaten, or even kill off? They may be silly habits and patterns and ways of seeing, but they are *my* cute and pathetic habits and patterns and ways of seeing. They are comfortable.

But you cross anyway, because you're not going for just comfort, but for Life, your Whole Self, because everything up to this point has prepared you for the journey. Some mysterious longing brought you here, to this very threshold. You may not know what is around the next switchback, but you know you will greet it with all you have— you are on the right path. It might not be *their* path, but it is *yours*.

The paradox is: you already aren't the same person that is taking that first step. They say the ceremony begins the moment you commit to it. And yet there's something about enacting the visceral visitation of each paw print along the path that gets that truth in you down in the bloods and bones.

So with a bright trust, we step onto the path, we cross over the threshold, with dedicated feet and an eager heart.

Intention

Intention can be an important part of crossing the threshold during a wilderness rite-of-passage, a life change, or any liminal transition, including our current Collective Initiation. Whatever collective initiation we are undergoing as a species or culture, it requires both dying to old forms that got us into this mess in the first place, and honoring the gifts and energies that are alive and here that will help shape whatever is emerging.

Intention is not necessarily a goal. It's good to have goals—they can be core parts of the journey. For example, "I am going to write two pages a day for a month; this month I am going to finish X amount of Y; I am going to look at the relationship with my parents." Or at the social or political level: "We will reduce our carbon footprint by 50% within 10 years; everyone will have a guaranteed basic income."

Yet Intention is performing something different than a goal. It is not so much a proclamation of future action, as worthy as they may be, but a recognition and honoring of what is, and what is emerging. It is a species of presence that authentically names what is already here—in us, in life.

It can be hatched as an "I am" statement: "I am a compassionate person who brings gifts of X to the community." Or "I am a woman who honors her body, rhythms, and boundaries in order to love herself and the world deeply."

Affirming. Evocative. Honoring.

Yet, even that way of carrying intention can retain flavors of exclusively human design, if it is unhitched from deeper truth, namely—Mystery.

We can call it the Threshold of Unrelenting Mystery.

If there's one thing confirmed over and over upon crossing the threshold, whether personal or collective: things unfold beyond our prediction and control. The other-than-human world hums along and we are but one syllable of a bigger conversation. A fierce wind blows things out of us; a shooting star elicits awe; a fire devastates; a fox touches you; lies we've been performing die.

Mystery will have its way.

These encounters transform us beyond anything we plan or intend. And they continue to work us long after.

Practicing the beautiful devastation of not-knowing can subsidize the journey. A sweet surrender is an attitude worth cultivating. Before the next footstep, uttering, "I don't know" and "I am open to listening" can go a long ways towards allowing things that might ordinarily be closed to our perception. As a whisper at first, perhaps; as a roar if we find the brutal truth of it in our belly.

Again this is equally applicable to the individual journey as to the cultural. Only then might we inhabit our proper place in the symphony of beings. Our niche in the ecosystem of repair. As a poem puts it, "How might we become a serviceable conduit for Mystery, for the world that is emerging?"

Instead of crossing clutching a bouquet of wants, what if we stepped over with the question the poet David Whyte asks:

What's the largest conversation we can have with the world?

Trust the Ceremony, Fuck the Ceremony, Trust the Ceremony

The first time I heard some version of the phrase "Trust the Ceremony, Fuck the Ceremony" was during my first wilderness fast with School of Lost Borders. My memory scratches in the desert dust of this, but I recall both inimitable guides, Betsy Perluss and Dr. Scott Eberle, uttering some version of it.

I had signed up for this ceremony six months before my birthday, which happened to be the first day of the program. Since registering and arriving on the land, my life had shapeshifted considerably, turned upside down. Yes, it was the disintegrating goo stage of the caterpillar's transformation. They say the ceremony begins the moment you say yes, and in those six months my psyche seemed to want to prove the truth of that.

In the intervening years, I too have adopted it as a motto for holding not only the wilderness fast rite-of-passage, but increasingly as a way of practicing living. Ceremony here can mean actual ceremony or ritual. Or in the largest sense it can signify Life, when approached ceremoniously and with sacred play and celebration. It is a way of honoring each season internally and externally.

The middle part, "Fuck the Ceremony" may sound sacrilegious, but is naming and honoring that very important and very human phase: things fall apart, break down, the part when you realize things aren't under your control, no matter how much you planned, no matter how much you rehearsed. As one of the poems here puts it, "I had my plans, and coyote pissed all over them."

This middle part is where Trickster energy lives. Where monsters come. When things dissolve, where you step in shit, where not a damn thing seems to go right.

The ways your old selves die over and over will surprise you. As Larry Hobbs was fond of reminding us, Stephen Foster always said "No one gets out of here alive." It's the part where confusion, doubt, uncertainty, anger, resentment, pettiness, shadow, and grief greet us with their beautiful and terrifying gigantic waves. Where the voices of giving up can live.

Of course, we often don't feel they're beautiful at the time. That can only arrive when we ALLOW them to speak their truth. A certain humility and surrender surfaces - if you're paying attention to the fact that this ain't just your show.

We often want nothing to do with all this. But...it's there nonetheless. There's a reason the Ceremony is often referred to as an Ordeal.

In my case, I was forced to reckon with my own inadequate structures and commitments to others. I was invited into a brush with death so I could excavate my own rooted values in high relief, like obsidian shards in the desert floor. I was so in "The West", or my own shit, I ended up putting my own life at risk, and as a result, putting the program at risk. In searching for healing of original wounds, I got stuck in the canyon on the wrong side of the mountain. The story of that is better told via the poems in the "Fuck the Ceremony" section below.

As another poem puts it: "Some give a wedding walk / wearing a desert gown / holding hands with themselves / for the first time/ carrying a bouquet of sagebrush / and desert tea / Others need a funeral march / with a torn mountain cloak / anointing themselves / with blood and sweat / holding hands with death / and a bouquet of heart-shaped rocks."

Why some require a funeral march and some adopt wedding vows is not known by humans.

In my case, this monumental sidetrack during my ceremony became the soil that grew every subsequent treasure that blessed my life.

Difficulty and some species of metaphorical death seem to be the two-step jig in the middle of the dance of transformation. Just ask the caterpillar/butterfly.

Often we resist what is most needed. We resist— We resist until we don't.

With each turn of the spiral, we come into remembrance that these are often necessary phases within the growth. They are core nutrients required for life's continual renewal and re-aligning.

Indeed, they are sacred energies for life. What if we approached them this way?

Surrender arrives on a bigger wave and in time we can grow into holding the "Fuck the Ceremony" softly within the bookends of that initial naive trust and a second, grander, more robust Trust.

This second kind of trust has teeth and bones in it. It's earthy, cosmic, and sometimes wily. It's a trust full of patience and compassion, sprouted in part from having been in and out of the canyon many times. It carries grit in one hand, grace on the other. It's something that Elders - that endangered species – often seem to not only possess, but exude.

And it is one rooted in a longer temporal frame— beyond the anxieties and freneticism of our current crises. It has Deep Time on its side.

We might call it Deep Green Trust.

May the poems included here be nourishment for others going on the sacred mountain to mark a transition, to claim their truth, to release the old, and live into their wild purpose, to bring beauty and medicine back to a world in need.

Trust the Ceremony

Fuck the Ceremony

Trust the Ceremony

TRUST THE CEREMONY

Arrive

Arrive just as you are.

Arrive here empty,
arrive here full of all the sick and stuck,
with all your love and longing,

your genius grief and gratitude

thick as your last tantrum.

Arrive here with your untainted pleasure
of being in your own skin,
of being skinned alive daily
but still showing up

Arrive here dripping wet with purpose,
arrive here awkward and awry
or full of awe

Arrive here without a sales pitch
but a blank check
to purchase the single now
with the wealth of your precious attention.

Arrive here in the slow pulse
of your becoming undone, and done in
by the best gesture you can summon
of surrender to the sacred why
that pierced you at birth
aiming you towards wider and wider circles.

Arrive here, allying with Water
following its promise to flow.

Ally with Sky, to widen
the palette.

Ally with Fire,
to stoke the passion
the world so desperately needs.

Ally with Earth,
to root in our true home.

We've got a lot of work to do.

We've got a lot of play to do.

Arrive here.

Arrive here.

Arrive here.

Desert Doorway

I came across the doorway of an ordinary poem, one made of dreams deep in the wild. I stepped through its threshold of purpose and arose a different being.

It's only a matter of deep time
before your dreams come to claim you.

To see how you might hold them.

It's not up to you how they decide to arrive.

It's only for you to decide
to unrust your hinges and enter or not.

Every doorway is a threshold—the limen,
in Latin.

That bottom part of the door
giving us the word liminality,
the betwixt and between,
passage between two stages.

We sever to make space for what is arriving.

Outside to inside and vice versa.

Sometimes what is leaving
is also what is arriving—
but shapeshifted with a new look in its eyes.

They might be our own.

That crossing is the key—Magic happens here.
All the good deaths and births acquire flesh.

To live in the door of the moment,
knowing everything is perpetual departure
and everything is perpetual arriving.

We the Yearning Ones,
live for tender intervals

thin as new feathers,
thick as a feast of hearts.

That's Threshold Living.

Walk Away, Invisible One

Walk Away, Invisible One,
take your place upon the land

Let your heart swell
as big and wide as the sky

Let the mystery of who you are
dance with the mystery of the mountain

When you are ready,
pick up a prayer

What does a prayer look like?

It may look like a naked dance
courting the soul of the world

It may look like collecting bones to sing over
or blowing embers in the palm of your hands
as gifts to a wounded world

It may feel like stewarding the storm within
towards the blossoming of a river lotus
at moonrise

It might sound like
a conversation with rocks and lizards
and other citizens of the canyon

It may sound like a song of gratitude,
rising unexpectedly from your belly
reclaiming joy

or the beat of a drum
forgetting who is drumming whom

or, it may sound like Silence

heard only by the Whale Ear
of Deep Listening

It may look like abandoning the old temples
to build the new ones

shedding skin and tears
that no longer serve
giving it back to the land as offerings

It may look like a question mark
in the form of a crooked juniper tree, asking:

Are you ready to commit?

Maybe you become a mouse
getting into the smallest spaces
to gnaw through bonds
that would have you bound

Or a funeral conductor, burying old stories

Or maybe you've become a warrior
taking a stand with blood pulsing,
announcing to the mountains:

"I'm here!"

Door-To-Mystery-Knows-Where

There is a door to Mystery-knows-where
and you are being invited to step through

The new doorway through which you pass
is framed with grander questions

where you'll pick up pieces left
in your canyons long ago

and find on the side
fragments resting by the fire

drinking ale for an evening tale
of dreams wanting to find their flesh

Put them in your wide-brim hat
and home in on your succulent belonging

becoming an obsessionate one
like a convict who loves their fate

This is the door to Mystery-knows-where
and you are being invited through

Tender Beauty of the Breakdown

This is a poem that came through during my first wilderness fast.

The sacred land is calling.

'Tap, tap, tap'
the bell beneath the breastbone beckons:

Come, be naked and empty
under the big sun.

Empty yourself of everything.

Empty of food, empty of distraction,
empty of ego, empty of old story.

For truer stories want to find their place.

Stretch yourself horizon to horizon
of your true home

until your soul image pops out
in high relief

like shards of obsidian
from the floor of the earth

Dive deep into your Great Sea,

into the Mariana Trench
of your unadorned self.

The cracking begins.

Like scorched soil
ready to receive.

The mud at the bottom of your being.

The shell of all the false identities.

Your fortressed heart—Cracked.

Oh it hurts—what gorgeous pain is this?

Die to all worlds
to which you don't belong,

leaving them to drift in the sage wind
as offerings to the land.

Cherish this tender beauty of the breakdown
and the sweet beauty of the rebirth.

Desert Vows

Some say the ceremony really begins
when tears fall into the desert dust

like a long-awaited thunderstorm
releasing all the heavy, old stories

and ends with tears of joy
swelling like the waxing moon

which is how Life committing to itself
looks on the face

Some give a wedding walk
wearing a desert gown

holding hands with themselves
for the first time

and carrying a bouquet of sagebrush
and desert tea

Others need a funeral march
with a torn mountain cloak

and anoint themselves
with blood and sweat

holding hands with death
and a bouquet of heart-shaped rocks

and still others dance
the celebration and the grief

The Great Sun shines on all
with equal regard

the Great With-ness to the vows
which are the same for all:

Thou shall not abandon thyself

Do you take/give this Beloved,
exquisite creature of the earth
to have/give and to hold lightly,
in this and every moment,
for better, for worse, for richer, for poorer,
in sickness and in health,
until death do us transform?

With an exchange known only
in the bones of the land

and the well-spring of the heart
a **Yes** is born once again

A Dis-/Per-/Con-Cussion

The Ceremony begins with a thump
on the head

You take a drumming
and the beat begins

Music swells with anticipation

You join the march of the beastly brigade:

the ranks are swollen
with trickster foxes and falcon outlaws
crossed-eyed rattlesnakes
and mischievous martens

every marmot and varmint
scoundrel, sinner and rascal insect
the regular army wouldn't accept

and you better believe
they ain't in it for the pay
or because it looks good on the resumé

Your feet thumps the trail
and the trail thumps you open
like a valley

A swollen skull soars
in skies swollen with ash

with whom you can have
no reasonable discussion

You don't yet know it
but the real threshold
is at the bottom of pain and pulse

where you find the wisdom
of no escape

This is the key that unlocks your re-entry
into the great story

old and new voices come unbidden
swelling from the depths

teaching you things you never knew
you needed

simply because you chose to
be here now

saying YES
to the largest conversation
you can have with the world

Feeling empty and well-fed
well-shed and well-thread
defatted and elongated
chiseled and grizzled
with a kink for leaning in

you start an apprenticeship
to shadows and rainbows

as daredevil bats pour somersaults
into your sunset eyes

The Ceremony ends with a thump
on the heart.

Let the Mountain Carve You

I. SEVERANCE

Commodities, cold machine.

Inherited boxes and bags too small,
all the Gotta-haves and Gotta-bes.

Virtually there. The Chase
and The Shining Hamster Wheel.

Too full yet empty.

Duller than a balmy day
sharper than a winter gale
the slow and sucking dry.

All the lies will die.

II. THRESHOLD

With wind and water
carry your dark and playful discourse
up and over

letting the desert carve
monuments out of you
epiphytic and free.

With River itself take your counsel.

With mud and mushroom heed
the wondrous whispers.

Your tail prefers a winding path
and your face of love finds itself
inside the tide of deep time.

III. RETURN

You'd rather eat beetles.

Rather a lot of things than live falsely.

Will they understand?

Once upon a time
you knocked on the wrong moon

but then hitched a ride
with a wild wind, your ears
to the ground of your being

finding that belonging is not a place
but a skill honed with a fierce heart.

You shift shapes from mountain pass
to alley way.

What is hidden remains your treasure.

What is visible becomes a sword and flute
—offerings to the numb ones.

And when you live your preposterous names,
into the world–

Oh how it ripples on and on.

Species of Surrender

Sometimes you must throw the flag of surrender.

Like Madrone surrendering their skin,
like Sky giving up
its vast accumulation.

Like Winter release
prostrating to the Great Seasoner
carrying dark green trust in open hands

knowing surrender is a secret password,
a life-luring dance on the skeleton
of thin agendas.

Like the mouse surrendering to talons above
in order to learn how to fly.

Sometimes you are invited to surrender
purity and knowing
as a pre-requisite for deeper intimacies.

To surrender to your own unfurling.
To surrender to the Unfathomable We.

To surrender to the dissolution,
But also to the integration.

All of which is forbidden
by the laws of man and Empire

Yet what might happen if you pitch
your strange curiosities tent
at the festival of slow surrendering?

If you placed all your delicate
and weaponized strategies
for anxiety management
at the threshold

and stand in the radiant darkness
hips open, arms a-twirl,
and heart akimbo?

Surrendering to the whispers of delicious dreams?

Surrendering to the frail and extravagant
Mystery of it all?

Make a Ceremony of It

It's time to die.

Which is to say, resurrect
the new season of you.

You know it's time
because that weight
you've been carrying around
in your chest

is no longer a treasure.

Because the inherited sacred stories
have all become tall tales.

Because the egg that cracked in you
birthed that golden bird
but hasn't built its new nest yet.

Because debris has accumulated
and there's not enough space
for the Big Grin—
the shape your heart makes
when all the sunspots are cleared.

Don't worry, death is not
what it used to be.

Just ask Earth
about its relentless pinking
and purple petaling.

Its gregarious greening

is nearly unbearable

and just like it, who you are
keeps surfacing

whether you want it to
or not.

But not first without
the exquisite requisite—

the slow sloughing off
of stale skin of seasons past.

Nothing's meant to last.

Not youth or bloodless truths
or all the yous
no longer you.

So honor the hour
and allow the old
to die well with "wow!"

making a ceremony of it
with a bow towards its corpse
and a bow towards the clearing

where your new season is arriving.

Dust On Her Feet

She sits on a sheepskin rug
crafted by her own Italian-made hands

digging in the dirt with a sagebrush stick,
declaring she's so tired of taking

With a scratch on her arm, dust on her feet
mud on her chest, fire in her heart

she exposes herself
with gifts of song

fire and laughter
and glimmering beads of seashell

we all share jicama
that makes our faces jump
because our taste buds are as confused

as the birds were
when the moon covered the sun

But she's as clear as the morning star
lifting up the desert day

a testament to rebirth
and commitment to making beauty

as an offering
to the wilderness within

No Lies On the Mountain

There are no lies on the mountain

On the mountain
there's no sales pitch

no ego, no image

rain is wet
sun is hot
snow is cold
rock is hard

things are what they are

You can't change it
nor does it want to change you

(though it just might)

It is implacable
yet not stubborn

It doesn't tell you what to do
or what to be

who you are
arises unadorned
like shards of obsidian
out of the earth

It Just Is

The mountain is one giant rock
one impenetrable I AM

whose body consists of
a billion and one different I AMs
of every possible hue, shape, and texture

Is that not the way of all things?

The mountain supports your every step
meeting you where you are

it pounds you with every step
meeting you where you are

Rocks refresh you
with their smooth, cool morning faces

Yet burn you
with their sharp, afternoon tongues

Rocks appear as hearts
and daggers pointed at your heart

Stones lift your sorrows
with their strong shoulders

and can crush your limbs and spirit
with their unrelenting gravity

Rocks feed your body and soul,
but as much as you try
you cannot drink a rock

any more than you can drink
the sweet western wind at dusk

The mountain is not your ally
nor is it your enemy

it just is—
how refreshing

Stone Buddies

When people are out on solo wilderness fast, they buddy-up. Each day they go to the buddy location, one in the morning, one in the afternoon, typically half way in-between solo spots, and mark in some way to indicate they are okay. It can be as simple or elaborate as they decide, some do nature art, some simple stone stacking. This is a poem honoring this beautiful simple ritual.

It's so simple, really, this raw ritual–

Two stones
stacked.

Then unstacked.

It's what ties us to the world
reminding us that we aren't out here

only for ourselves.

My buddy is the stacker
in the morning

I'm the unstacker in the afternoon.

He leaves watercolor portraits
of the eastern mountains

over and around which

dawn shuffles in with impossible pinks
and persimmons, a citrus buffet.

In return, I leave poems, hoping to tell the truth.

It's a movement full of grace,
perhaps a template for other exchanges:

authentic, generous, reciprocal.

I don't know how the days are dancing
within him

or if he is tracking the nights like I do

as Mars commutes for twelve hours
horizon to horizon.

But I know he will receive what he needs

and bring it back to the world
as medicine.

As will I.

This Breath

The parts of me that are steep
you shall soon know

From here the valley
looks like one dark green
folding tattoo of belonging

and it will take your breath away

then give it back.

Soon enough
we'll get to the final breath

but this breath is reserved for being

a breath spent on passion perhaps
or a silent prayer

The valley needs the peak-point-view
and the mountain needs the valley-eyes

just as the out-breath
needs the in-breath

But don't abandon yourself
down there

nor float away like a cloud
forgetting your dark red root

Let's be big like Gaia
in her all-season robes

naked as her starkest desert

This breath now is a sigh of wonder

stepping off the high mountain nest
and finding finally how wind
is your fiercest ally
and moon your elder

your mentors since the first cry
on the first day

as everything is, you realize

when your husky eyelids dissolve
like mist under this bold new sun

Knock and See What Answers

How you know yourself
like the taste of blood in your mouth

like desire ripe as guardian oak—
crimson and certain.

To share this and find yourself knowing anew
with a fabulously defeated mind.

It starts as a look—something befuddled
has your face in the water
drinking a startled pulse of meaning.

Knock and see what answers.

Wait patiently.
Do not force your way in.

Sit on the porch of your own horizon 'til dawn
if you must.

Maybe it's your porch.
Have you checked your basement, your attic?

Maybe it's your house and you forgot the key.

Maybe the key has been hidden
under the chair you've been sitting on
this whole time.

Unlock your desire, taste your blood.

Don't lose heart, the night is young.

FUCK THE CEREMONY

Juniper Dreams and Piñon Nightmares

There's a sagebrush burning
beneath my breastbone
casting off sparks of juniper dreams
and piñon nightmares

my mind's racing like a desert hare,
but can't catch up
with the tortoise of my soul

'I' have a plan,
but my plan has a plan

so I just cast a curious glance
squinting like the crescent moon

curious about who is stalking my dreams
like a canine con artist

"Yip, yip, yip!"

He sniffs into my dreamshed
and pisses on my precious plans

I've been coyote'd
and even the lizards are laughing
as they linger
under red rocks

That crusty corvid
snarls from the twisted tree top:

"Come this way...
if you dare...

Sure, bring your intent,
but drop your goals
in the dust.

Boy do we have a surprise for you…"

Sidewinding Ceremony

*The darker the eyes, the further we see,
slithering down in a slithery spree,
slithering up, slithering free.*

It's a gift to be thwarted on the path
and have your straight arrow bent
by the sidewinding ceremony
of falling out of time on dirty knees

you notice there's no place to stand
where you aren't permeated
by other worldings

Saturated by surplus surprises
you hear the call to crawl crookedly

to find your flicker
and sprout scales

in order to be recognizable
to those who live inside a different pace

building otherwise allegiances
with each colubrine council
and chthonic conversation

How else to notice who else is here?
How else to notice when else is now?

How else to be welcomed
into the parliament of voices

and enlisted by a different dream?

Wound and Not the Story of the Wound

From that high place
it appears a lake

pinkish-white and round with promise
a beautiful mark on the land
walled in by red rock
and a giant sky

It asserts itself on me
draws me like a fish fishing
a man, thrashing

You'd think a part of me
would know about mirages
in the desert

But I need to touch
the wound
and not the story of the wound

So I begin the descent
with no dragons or wizards
or helpers other than lizards
and my companions:

Death and all my loves

we say the unspoken things
that need to find a purchase
in the open air

so it could float on up
and meet the sun

Too far, too far.
No, go the distance.

Which powers in me were having this debate?

I climbed down
sliding over sandstone,
through shadows and stories

find and give forgiveness
empty stomach, full of purpose

Too late to turn back now
I must touch the wound
not the story of the wound

Arriving at the day's brutal center
thirst stretches out like dune devils

sun hovers an inch from my forehead
like a rune foretelling troubling things

My feet find cracked mud.

It is no lake. It is not pink, nor soft,
but white as a skeleton.

The only water comes from my face
forced by the realization:

the stories, my false god
how much I'd wasted with stories
of the wound
and not the wound itself.

I bless it with the final tear.

Dry, renewed, I turn
towards the arduous ascent

swollen tongue, swollen heart
with my companions:

Death and all my loves, now
including myself

Note: The phrasing of the title of this poem is influenced by Wallace Stevens's Not Ideas About the Thing but the Thing Itself and Adrienne Rich's Diving Into the Wreck:
the thing I came for:
the wreck and not the story of the wreck
the thing itself and not the myth

The Shape of Death, The Shape of Life

Sometimes the way you think love
abandoned you

takes the shape of a shimmering lake
in the desert

miles from safety,
miles from reason.

But you must go anyway
in order to find the real shape

to find the final tear
and in order for the final tear to fall

you must fall
further than all the times before.

So you walk step by severe step
descending dry and deep

walking hand and hand with death,
your first ally.

You walk tenderly
with regret and forgiveness
with love and release

You tell all of them goodbye

You keep falling
further than the times before

until you discover the lake is a mirage
and always has been

And the desert takes its due
and the sun is not, in fact, your ally

The ways you believe love abandoned you
comes in the shape of a parched throat
and parched thoughts

but the truth wants to form a syllable
inside you
and it whispers your name

and you know now:
You abandoned yourself

And it hurts.

Everything.

Everything is on fire.

You are so thirsty.

The fire says, *die here or climb*.

It is not a koan—the fire means what it says:
Climb or die here now.

Fire is many things, but not a liar.

If you abandon yourself now once again
you abandon everywho you claim to love

You can't love
without surrendering yourself

into the Big Heart

So you begin.

Your body moves up the mountain
and there's nothing pulling you up
except one thought—

you have too much to give
to lie down here forever
under the big hard sun

The way love finds you
comes in the shape of hot heart rocks

the most beautiful things you've ever seen
that appear as you climb your way out

hand over fist
over hand over fist

claiming your life with everything
that is still alive in you

They are screaming your true names
with a strength beyond muscle

until finally, you reach the rim of the world.

The desert and the mountain
and the heart of the world
have tattooed the shape of love
in you

and you know now: you will never
abandon yourself again.

The Sky Is Blue

Ask me how I know the face of denial

Ask me how I know how it feels
to own eyes sewn wide shut
with parched lips dripping tales

how the mind smuggles in denial
like a shapeshifter fumbling to find
every crooked crack

desperate to defend
some same ol' same ol'
some story of self

ask me how I know
how denial places a hold on the heart

an act of resistance
to what is

until that sweet, sweet moment
when a sharp green truth marches in
like an unassailable enemy
who is really your best friend

when denial is denied
by that dead-end darkness
on the path you've been treading

showing you the only way out
is to become so completely lost
you try to drink rocks

There's only one way to walk now:

the sky is blue
you can't drink rocks

the sky is blue
I was wrong,
forgive me

the sky is blue
you can't eat the wind
the sky is blue

the mountain is you
many ways up but can't go through

the sky is blue
pain is here
many ways through but can't go around
the sky is blue

confusion is here
the sky is blue

self-betrayal is here
the sky is blue

can't grasp a cloud
the sky is blue

death stalks us all
the sky is blue

yes, forgiveness is here
life busts through

the sky is blue

everything is crooked and cracking

love is here
that's why it hurts

the sky is blue
you are the giveaway

the sky is blue

ask me how I know

At the Feet of That Brutal, Beloved Teacher

What does it mean to walk with death?

You can walk with death
as an act of imagination
having conversations with love
on the way to the death lodge

Don't think it's not there
just because you made it up

You can walk with death
as an uninvited guest
climbing hand over fist
with a closed throat
up the mountain

You can make of yourself an apprentice
at the feet of that brutal, beloved teacher
learning lessons sorely needed

knowing that fall lives in the spring seed.

For how can you really be here
saying hello to each moment
without a goodbye
on the tip of your tongue?

That is how to pray, it says,
the first and only lesson.

Finally, you can walk with death
as life's partner

hand in hand, allied
like a ripe citizen of the earth

with, if not praise, then respect
holding it gently to your heart

for this one who arrives at every hour
or any hour

So do not be surprised
by its walking onto the scene
with a beguiling smile

Praise will come later
when the heart swells beyond measure

For is that not the way
of each bright new petal

every astonishing sunset
taking your breath away?

Taking away all breaths
so there may be the new?

Each Inch Etches Something Holy

Smile, we say
to our broken sentences

throwing candy to keep us clutching
at the tried-and-not-so-true

Be brave, bold robot
our programming tells us

trying always to be a parade of boons
and unstained hope

What if from time to time
we allow our words free range

to be scared and sacred
wounds they point to

not mere scar tissue
but real, raw and open

to the risk of infection
by terrible truths

that have no interest in being buried
with the past or some species of denial

I don't know how to do it
but this poem wants to let it be

a slow pilgrimage
of love and lament

until the Earth
in us has felt heard

until the River
in us has felt beflowed

until we've heard the iceberg
in us mourn being hit

by the unwieldy ship of us
now too difficult to carry

until we've felt the Village
in us aching from being burnt

over and over and over
over and over...

yet even I, a talented grief-monger
can't seem to sustain such a march

can't open wide enough
can't get low enough on the ground

though knowing each inch
etches something holy

stitches together some garment
that we so long to wear

yet worry if we're worthy
of its wholeness

Language must do better,
I think, if Life is to be lured back

Perhaps by speaking devout words
in the shape of defenseless hearts

with each step
soft and surrendering

like
the
slowly
sinking
sun.

Stoned

So winter seized you up
for two years straight

or crooked–as truth would have it

and truth will have it
belching out how Trouble gnawed you raw

how a gargantuan grief grazed the grass
of you down to a stubble

Nothing against Winter—
we're believers in each turn

it's just that if the soil of us sleeps
long enough
it begins to forget its fecundity

and fashions as normal
a contorted shape

like the flat tire
of a wheelbarrow

that's never known fixing
or a fallow field bereft of tending

seasons aren't what they used to be
and you begin to shake, wondering:

is this how imperial mind could be
defeated, be
undone, be
turned over,
like a painted turtle

like a plow slicing a field
surfacing finally
the dark humus of what we need
for a mature crop of our kind to sprout?

you think two winters long is as thick
as smoke in the west
until you start spending time with stones

and by spending time, i mean hearing time
deep as death, a booming bass

as a rule, you've got to get low
and so slow your tortoise soul
outpaces your rabbit mind

to funnel in their elegant echoes
their hallowed whispers

and then, if you fall on your face
like a good citizen

you start picking up all your other seasons
start harvesting your colors

like impossible orange lichen
just reclining like an ancient god
on the surface of things

cradled by grandmothers of grandmothers

start picking up hints of how to hold
the ever-darkening times
in the sun-palm of your hands

until even an era is a moment
you learn to love

practicing the language of circles
the glistening grammar of stars
and berries alike

at once bursting with new
and ancient flavors of Life

So, Crack

Where you arrive at the end of one nation
and another begins,
they tell you

but where an old self ends
and a new one opens up

you must discover yourself
over and over
through vast experiments of trial and t(error)

The kind of (t)error that has you thinking
you're floating untethered
away from the space vessel
and all form of things

Or are you one who thinks you know
good from bad
when all the beautiful things seem to break?

When foundation Earth cracks
and space comes hurtling
through your bones?

Unravel more accurately
and sink into your silence
robust and cunning

but then, embrace the kind of uncertainty
that has you planting dreams
for the seventh generation

the kind that adds a layer of fat

to your empathic system

Yes, part of you wants to think
all the notes come up black

and part wants to keep plunging
past the comets
to make your own orbit

The part of you that,
like a meadow of wildflowers
wants into the world so bad
it will do anything to make it happen

including leaping lupine
and flashing fuchsia
petaling upward umbeled and spiked

Or do you really think that meadow arrived
gently on wings of peace?

What of the ten million year preamble
of terrible upheaval
anticipating the beauty before you?

So, crack.

Break into the liminal space
with all the elegant pain you can muster

Forget all the fine tethers,
attractive and dead

Even fish have to jump out of their world
from time to time

Turn indigo and crack the crust

petaling your meadowed self
without restraint

until your chasmly scream
and unbound love—
pure and unshackled—
booms through all the worlds

When It Booms From Below

It is not an indictment—
though it feels like one—
when the noise begins to ebb

and those first clear words
bubble up from your well
seasoned with deep time.

For eons you stayed busy,
for lifetimes ignored
the vowels of your own voice.

But when it booms from below
and floats to the surface
you know you must change your life.

It is tempting to whip
the back of your soul
for not knowing.

For forgetting.

But that is not
the hand of love.

Fine, you didn't know. You couldn't hear.

Fine, you abandoned yourself.

You abandoned lots of things.

You filled your ears with others' bells,
your eyes with ugly things.

You fueled your fears with storied spells,
your skies with wobbly wings.

That was yesterday. Not today.

Today you choose.

Now it begins—scoop up those strange sounds
and quench your ancient thirst.

A Ripe and Relentless Cracking

Look, I won't talk about it if you don't—
I don't want to hurt
so damn spiritually in front of anyone

To bear it is intolerable
this sacred wound which cannot be named

The one that shudders the body
writhing with entombed remembrances
when no one is looking

the one that has us so leashed and lashing
so narrowed and knotted

that it has us exiling our sweetest intimacies
has us doing just about anything
not to feel what's underneath

Yet these crooked questions keep crawling
to the surface of our blood:

What if that dark sweet amber pain
mistaken for trouble
is the next true step?

What could possibly bring us back
but a ripe and relentless
geo-mystical cracking?

We can keep the silence
or we can start squeaking
and making awkward gestures
toward each other

at first soft enough
we'll have to stretch our ears
to make sure it's not just a mouse
in the corner

then loud enough
that even now the seventh generation
is singing songs about it around the campfire

Caterpillar Dreams

"Slowly I crawl, feeding on life, blade by blade. On the edge, falling and feeding, can't stop eating, yet hungry all the time. I dream of impossible things.' Woolly Bear Caterpillar (Isabella Tiger Moth)

One piece of outrageous after another.

From predicting the winter to the staggering number of muscles in the head (248).

Fulfilling a sacred commandment:
Eat. Rest. Transform.

A voracious hunger. Never enough. Haunted and blessed by hints of a larger life.

An impossible dream of flight.

Then, an audacious act of cryo-magic—
freezing itself into the future

Is but preparation for a slow death.

And even slower resurrection.

If spring should arrive, a mythopoetic performance to rival the gods—

Through a daredevil Dance of Dissolution
a larval life liquefies.

Imaginal buds proliferate

surrendering to a surprise transformation.

No one could have predicted this.

Everyone will forgive the blackness necessary for the shapeshifting.

Everyone begins to wonder:

What root-wings are already here amidst the frantic feeding?

TRUST THE CEREMONY

Within Your Wings of Trickster Trusts

Courageous chirply birds of dusk
Please pull me out my heavy husk

To make of me as moonly must
Taking all my lavish lusts

Blowing all my settled dust
With your wings of trickster trusts

Guttural Utterance of Holy Unknowing

Be it not a prayer for more.

Forgo a petition or polyrhythmic pleading.

This is not asking for one more damn thing from Earth.

This is a guttural utterance of holy unknowing,
a shuddering body-gate of gratitude.

A permission to feel, disguised as an offering of redemptive nonsense.

A watershed shakedown of every last resistance.

A contraband clearing out smuggled in
as renegade riverside rhythms.

This is surrender and a cracked-ear heart.

A rainbow breath birthing grace.

This is an 'I'm here,'
opening my everything.

We Dream the Butterfly

You only have to ask the butterfly
that a cocoon can be a safe haven

but also a guardian against the truth
that is arriving, if you linger in the threshold

Yet it is the abode of transformation–
if we're willing to surrender and disintegrate

Willing to trust that there's nothing
more practical than dying and resurrecting

which are the basic operating instructions
of the universe

willing to trust that ink black uncertainty
is necessary for shapeshifting

Willing to trust the ceremony
of our old bodies dissolving
becoming root-wings of the new

Yes, becoming goo is brutal

but holding onto old forms
is even more painful

We are imaginal buds
of what is trying to emerge

no longer having allegiance
to the caterpillar of us

but to the dream of liberation.

Pollinating wildflowers,
birthing wild new prairies—

We dream the butterfly.

That Tide Your Heartbeat

Remember when you doubted?

Back in the season of smallness
when the Big Trust
was a secret password
known only to the society of saints?

Remember when your shallow image
peered back at you
from the distorted mirror of your tiny house?

And when you smashed that mirror
with a mountain heart

using the shards to carve some robust image
in the sands of time
that even mighty ocean could barely contain

the sun and moon
became your peers,
the tide your heartbeat.

And now—
now you dance

sometimes as the shoreline
sometimes as the sea

sometimes as the raindrops
on granite peaks

inhaling hardness
exhaling softness

with starlight falling
through your fingertips
and whole galaxies underfoot.

If Today Is Not the Day

I can show you where the old oak lives
but not what dialect is spoken there.

For that, you must sit with them and be a friend.

The canyon I fell into
and climbed back out of
is mine, not yours.

The up and the down of it
are well-earned creases
in my palms and around my eyes,
companions on the pilgrimage.

But they are not your ups and downs.

Your canyon has different contours,
sings different songs.

Don't follow me. Don't
follow me into the silent cave
or over green valleys with falcon eyes.

Follow your own bird in your own sky.
Carve your own cave and grab your own ears.

My way of knowing the sharp cry
from its beak, or how it soars
is my way, not yours.

If today is not the day
to trust your ancient whispers,
when is?

Trust, Beaver

As empty as a beaver skull—
that's how the big trust is
and as full as the life that got you here.

Not knowing when you'll be in the river
or beside it rotting.

Chew on life with your tremendous teeth
or let it gnaw you to bits–
your choice.

What do you want them to write on your bones?

Wild Syllable of Trust on Your Lips

There's absolutely no way
you can be a sun god
if you're not simultaneously a dung beetle.

You are no part-time lover—
there's no way to be one of the great lovers
without excavating your name
from the center of the earth

without pulsating the No-Name
from the center of the moment

the grand pulse hidden
in the Everything

No grand ascent without the dark
and mysterious descent.

No flying without digging.

You are not here to flee from parts of you
you think you can't meet in yourself.

So stand with arms outstretched
and a wild syllable of trust
on your lips

comprehensible only to those
with the great longing
pouring in and out
of their cracked ear hearts.

Next Time She Draws Blood

The next time she draws blood

will be double the draw
daring to double the trust

As trust is a sunrise
always showing up on time

For wild hearts are not misers
and blood does not deal
in fractions

but boldly pours itself
through the course of things

Or not at all.

Like light.

Trust is a Bright Star
or a Blackhole.

It's not about knowing it won't hurt

but knowing it will, and still
bearing your palms,
your chest,
your antecubitals, saying:

HERE I AM!

I have it to spare.

And that, my Dear Gambler,
is the dazzling difference between

the fine champagne of living
and the flat booze of withholding.

Circulation

Sometimes all you need
is the blessing of a deep summer moon

giving a sermon on change
and powerful secret things

Adopted by your heart
they circulate through you

even when the clouds conspire
to play hide and seek

Sometimes all you need
is marmalade sunset or impossible dawn

to circulate through you
like a solar system jamboree

Sometimes all you need
is the crisp mountain breath

the living wild offspring
of a million madrone and unending green

Adopted by your blood
they circulate through you

Sometimes all you need
are the smooth sounds of water

gliding and gulping
over glistening stones at the muddy creek

As a reminder of all the flowing things
circulating through you

Serviceable Conduit

Don't feel bad for having forgotten–
Feel more.

Don't get out your impressive whip
just because you fell asleep yet again

The world already believes
all-too-brightly in mandatory punishment.

Instead, say Yes
to mandatory astonishments
of a world bent on beauty.

Conduct research into surrendering
to skin-on-skin contact with Mystery.

Inquire into being a serviceable conduit
for what wants to be created through you.

Practice over and over
an abundant alignment
that longs to enflesh some wondrous thing

Offering your Life
in ceremonial commitment
to the Grand Metabolism.

Keep Walking, Visible One

When the prayer has fully prayed you,
Walk in, Visible One.

Take your place in the Circle—
it is time to be seen.

It is sometimes hard
to come down the mountain

But do not linger in the threshold.

We need your story.

Walk In, Visible One,
take your place in the World,

because the purpose of going out
is to come back.

Keep walking,
Keep making the beauty
giving it away as medicine

the beauty that is uniquely you
crafted in care like the smallest bead

that Earth and the people
so desperately need.

Keep walking, Initiated One,
Keep walking

Always Here

Why did you bring me here?
You are always here

at the beautiful cusp
of expansion and contraction

Yes, but why did you bring me here?
Why did *we* bring *us* here?

You see, it's all the Sea—
River, I trust your journey

What Preposterous Pulse pretending
to be a me

What Preposterous Pulse pretending
to be a you

How will you show up?
With dust on my feet

How will you show up?
With scratches on my skin

How will you show up?
With fennel on my breath

How will you show up?
With Ocean in my eyes

How will you show up?
Shoulder to the Wheel

How will you show up?
With playful paws

How will you show up?
With talons of love

How will you show up?
As the gravity of worms

How will you show up?
As the lightness of wings

How will you show up?
As a basket of silence holding all the noise

How will you show up?
Beastly and beriddled

Why speak in riddles?
Would you rather we not speak at all?

How will you show up?
Heartbroken and Whole

How will we show up?
Heartbroken and Whole
Heartbroken and Whole
Heartbroken and Whole

Spiraling Up (Cairns of Holy Longing)

A long path. Is it worth following to the end?

Gazing up it looks impossible.

The sheer scale of the thing
is dizzying

and if all you're accustomed to
are thin shoes and a habit of slipping

it's a lot easier to keep to the path
you've been walking.

But should your imagination
get the best of you

you might find there are several ways
to spiral up the mountain

all involving the same move:
space and a slow and steady pace

It's inevitable you'll become disoriented
from time to time

a certain panic or pain arrives
threatening to close you down

Clicks will emerge
and you might read them
as alarms

or perhaps you'll hear them as chirps

of your grasshopper heart
indicating something wants to be revealed

That's the moment to push
the pause button.

Look around. If you are patient
and cultivate a plumed heart

you'll start to see cairns
of holy longing

stacked as stones
along your highest path.

Who put them there is not known.
Maybe someone looking out for you—

Maybe it was you.
This may feel unfamiliar

being so used to the comfortable
dirty pain of collapse.

Yet the sun says
try something different:

Give your body the gift of air
and look around.

A cairn appears.
You give a step.

This is how it will be
with each turn:

Something will want to twist you
and something will invite you upwards.

There's no magic trick here.
Pause. Breathe. Look around. Give a step.

Practice this 40 or 50,000 times
and you'll be on your way.

A poet once said,
a lover learns to leap.

"Nothing risked, nothing gained,
razzle dazzle, play the game…"

Yes, a lover leaps, but first
a lover must get their footing.

If you are committed to going fast
mistakes are guaranteed

A lover leaping with a pocket full of wounds
is just another reckless fool

or worse, liable to bring a boulder down
on the whole thing.

And best believe, once a boulder has landed
chances of recovery are slim.

Pause. Breathe. Look around. Give a step.

Opportunities to spiral down
are always there.

You'll know it because that familiar tug
would have you cursing

blaming even the rocks
and calling the wind names.

Pause. Look around.
Give the next right step

towards the cairn
of your holy longing.

Give your body
the gift of air.

You'll reach a point
where you'll look back

seeing all the places below
where you've let your spiral down

the devastated landscapes you walked
the fires you've started

You'll swell with a tender surrender
in the recognition the damage is done

Yet even then, a view as soft
as the stone is hard

makes the next cairn
materialize out of nowhere.

There is room for mourning
but there is no room for punishment

and so you give a breath
and you give a step

dedicating them both to Mystery.
There will be a point

where there's nothing left to do
but scramble on your hands and knees

sweating and surrendering.
So forget dignity—

This is not a pissing contest, this is not
about fucking mountain climbing.

This is about something much harder—Love.

You give a step and suddenly find yourself
in a clearing

with so much space
it feels like you can see forever

feels like you could fit
whole mountain ranges inside

And just when you think you've arrived
the wind picks up

carrying on its wings
a falcon in ever-widening gyres

hinting that the spiral is unending
and requires a heart as light as a feather.

For now, it is enough to know
it is time to bring the spiral home.

The Experiment Isn't Over

What if we don't really know
if the universe is expanding
or contracting

or both?

because we don't know
how willing or able we are
to stay open

We ask ourselves:

Can I withstand the crunch?

What if like a buried seed
the real question lurking is:

Can I bear the sound
of my shell cracking open

with that sweet amber pain
mistaken for trouble?

Our ears pick up
the warbler's woo

suggesting dawn is here
yet again

and we breathe a little deeper

Suggesting these cycles
are built into everything

Suggesting the experiment
isn't over

The Path Is Made

We're returning.

There is no path, pilgrim.

The path is made by crawling and clawing.

The path is made by climbing.

The path is made with caresses.

The path is made with compassion.

The path is made by contradictions.

The deeper we crawl, the brighter we burn.

Start crawling.

Mix the kernel of your truth—
that improbable spark
in the vastness—

with the clay of where you live,
deep with dreams.

It is your own dawn
looking Earth in the face
saying, "I remember you"

It is a longing long in seed form
worth a watering.

We're returning.

On the North Face It

On the north face of it
things are different—

That it carries the world's
frost and shadows and excess fur

is not something they teach you
in dream school

where it's all about the big vision
and the grand view from the mountain top

Yes, hidden horizons are glimpsed
from the most northerly nest

where the sun never sets
and a vast circle forms inside you

But true north also touches on textures
tucked away from dalliance with daylight

bringing together the softest
with the grittiest

the discarded
with the desired

where the soul of the smallest mushroom
and beasts robust enough

to embrace the harshest winter
are the same thing

It speaks in unlikely pairings of opposites
because its native tongue is both/and

and having become fluent
in paradox

it holds the four directions in its mouth
the Great Turning in its lap

Cupcake Buffaloes

Cupcake Buffaloes is the name of my wilderness ceremony guide training cohort, taken from a story my guide Larry Hobbs told about his mentor telling him he could either continue the despairing habits he was wallowing in or go down and spend time with a bison named Cupcake. After much hemming and hawing, he went down and found a magnificent beast, standing in the wind and cold, frost forming on its beard, weathering the winter storm, together with the herd. It jarred him into getting his act together. Or at least that's how I remember the story.

We're all in it now–
Fires and uncertain skies
Breathing in ash kin and breathing out sighs

There's no fleeing any more.

Somedays the sun doesn't come up
and we each must decide:

How will I *be* with this collapse?
How will I help pull the sun up with *my* gifts?

But we cupcake buffaloes
turn our faces towards trouble

because we've learned the hard way
the wisdom of no escape

It's not that our hearts too aren't utterly broken
it's that a savage pulse lives within us

unwilling to let the big lie of separation
have the final word

And yes, it asks of us more than we think
we can handle sometimes

But the seasons have seasoned us
shaking wholeness from us
with each tremendous turning

We've learned well from ancestors
and Ant-Sisters,

Brother Pine
and we keep our ears open for Elder Wind

Look, the people are hurting
Earth is screaming

A vast forgetting has us all by the throats

But a lover learns to leap
and shows up with gifts and a brave shoulder

A lover learns to listen
and shows up with an unconditional caress

just as the new rain quenches
a parched land

And we cupcake buffaloes,
bovine revolutionaries,
are lunatic lovers of the world

and so we say—as much to them
as to ourselves—

place your sacred rage
and tender tears
into the circle on the wild mountain

Come with your holy uncertainty
and body abuzz with both grief and joy
as oblation to the land

All is welcome here–
We won't find spring without them.

So we drop our bellies low to the center
a hoof in each direction
and utter into the whipping wind:

We're here
We're here
We're here

The Ceremony Is Messy and Perfect

Letting bees buzz across every last inch
of your inner landscape—
that was the ritual.

To weigh your heart
against a feather, even though
you've been eating rocks.

The rattle is shaking—
who is rattling whom is not always clear.

We didn't count the stars
that night to go to sleep.

We didn't sleep at all.

The stars strained their necks in curiosity
at what we were up to.

Though they should have known,
having burst into their own destiny
over and over again.

Step one, die.

Die to old selves no longer needed—Slough off
the dead tissue from your living flesh.

Step two, cross the threshold
of desire
into your Unfathomable.

Step three, Return—
Your face will look different.

Your eyes say something new.

And whatever your heart weighs now,
only you and the wind know.

Humor and humility will be added
to your vocabulary

with dirt under your fingernails
of your last defense

You may pronounce love
with a different accent.

The ceremony is messy and perfect.

The ceremony will birth a thousand stories.

The ceremony will never end.

EPILOGUE

Many folks arrive on the land or approach the experience expecting that to be the most challenging aspect. But it is The Return, the Incorporation stage that can be site of the most struggle. In large part because now we are invited to embody all that we had insight into, the conversations we had with the world, the visions that visited, the gifts we claimed.

Yet the world is still the world—it hasn't had your conversation, nor does it seem to honor much the sacred things—and we will be tempted over and over to fall asleep, to fall into old forms and habits, to forget. We will be tempted to think all that we experienced out there as something like a dream.

And this is where the Ceremony will find its throughline. Or not.

We will be invited to re-member our sagebrush stories and all the shimmering specks that called us home.

Does a Little Speck Remain?

Who has the eyes to see
the feral paw prints
still tracking across your heart
as the world races into the future?

Have all the sharp voices already
drowned out that clarion call
clear as the morning star
pulling up the sun?

Who has the ears to hear
your sagebrush story
of death and rebirth
growing in your gut
as the world rolls on?

Who has the time
for a trickster moon
howling in your bones
as the world floats on by?

Who can feel the warmth
of a juniper bark fire still blazing
beneath your breastbone
as the world turns?

Have all the rough rags
of the routine
already washed you clean
of your magic mountain dust?

Or does a little speck remain?

Does a bright song abide
within the heartbeat
of your delicious desert dawn?

If so, let it be the seed note
of your sacred symphony
sprouting through the concrete
of the world
as it pours itself along your path

ABOUT THE AUTHOR

Ryan Van Lenning, M.A., is author of *Re-Membering: Poems of Earth and Soul*, *One Bright and Real Caress*, *From Inside These Wild Ones*, and a collection of haiku, *High-Cooing Through the Seasons*. His new collections, *An Ambitious Silence* and *Becoming Beautiful Barbarians,* will be released throughout 2025-26. He is the 2019 recipient of Jodi Stutz Poetry Award by Toyon Literary Magazine and his poetry appears in various poetry journals and the book *A Walk with Nature: Poetic Encounters That Nourish the Soul* and *Behind the Mask: 40 Quarantine Poems from Humboldt County*. He facilitates 6-week workshops called Write Your Wild River, Earth Intimacies, and Deep Belonging in the Great Turning a couple times a year.

Ryan is founder of Wild Nature Heart, supporting people to re-connect with the wisdom of both inner and outer wild nature, to live their callings into the world, and to assist in the work of repairing broken belonging during this collective initiation. He is a teacher, ecotherapist and wilderness rite-of-passage guide and lives among the forests and rivers of Northern California.

ABOUT WILD NATURE HEART

Wild Nature Heart supports people to connect with the wisdom of inner and outer wild nature, to embody our wholeness, and to live our wild purpose into the world in order to inhabit our particular niche in the ecosystem of healing and justice. Through 1-on-1 earth-rooted mentoring, custom and group wilderness rite-of-passage ceremonies, and various courses, workshops, and seasonal gatherings, Wild Nature Heart cultivates an ecospirituality that nourishes our deep belonging in the animate web of life in order to do the decolonial work that we are called to do in this moment of the Great Turning.

Wild Nature Heart believes that to cross this threshold into species maturity with a next-season guest pass we must keep our imaginations robust and make moves that subvert inherited paradigms of fear and supremacy. We are being invited to fall through the inherited maps into new territories towards collective liberation. As crises continue to invite us across thresholds of initiation, we crack open the paved highways of our hearts and bodies to allow the tributaries of our holy longings and wild purpose to flow in and out.

The journey is both a daily and life-long practice, as much as it is multi-generational and multi-species. We practice simultaneously being both death doulas to the world that is dying and birth doulas to the one being born.

www.wildnatureheart.com

TITLES IN THE *RE-MEMBERING* SERIES

Re-Membering: Poems of Earth and Soul

The 75 poems in *Re-Membering* are an unabashed celebration of the sensuality of wild nature. Redwoods reach without apology towards the sky, and rivers flow with unflagging energy towards the ocean. This collection re-members Ryan's personal explorations into wild nature, but it also re-collects for all of us a time when our kinship and inter-connectedness with the natural world was self-evident, and invites us to fully re-inhabit and say "Yes!" to our sensual natures, our animal bodies, our playfulness and creativity, connection, mystery, and our instinctive love for this beautiful, sentient Earth.

"Ryan's poetry speaks deeply and clearly to the awakening to our true interconnected nature, which is the only way we can transform our world."—Molly Young Brown, author of *Coming Back to Life: The Updated Guide to the Work That Reconnects* (co-authored with Joanna Macy)

One Bright and Real Caress

Build an altar at each moment with a goodbye on the tip of the tongue.
Slow dance drunk in the robust now.
Show up with playful paws and the gravity of worms.
Strap the searchlight around your ribs and shuffle like a crescent moon over all your little resistances.
Saunter past all the gates.
Slit yourself down the middle, pull your skin to the horizon and drip like a mountain.
Can we be here now? Really be here?

These are some of the invitations lurking in the poems of One Bright and Real Caress. This collection is a celebration of the moment. Of not escaping. Of impermanence. Of death as life partner. With syllables of relentless affirmation, these poems bring an unconditional caress over all the textures of life and our multitudes within. As an invitation to presence and an honoring of the all-too-real struggle to not flee the moment, *One Bright and Real Caress* welcomes every conceivable crescent mood, slivered and slow, with no aim but to edge out more and more into the whole ceremony and celebration.

One Bright and Real Caress is Book 2 in the Re-Membering Series.

From Inside These Wild Ones

From Inside These Wild Ones is a collection of earthy poetry emerging from the author's experiment of living outside with the seasons and the living sky as his heart-home roof. From bears, bees, and birds, to storms, snakes, and silence, these poems honor the animate web of life and our intimate relationship inside it. The poems here are not only reminders of the mystery of our other-than-human kin, but evocations of the animals we are. These 77 poems weave lyric, humor, and mythopoetic exploration to invite a multispecies, embodied, and soulful participation in the unfolding symphony of life. The beasts within are lurking, listening, yearning to live.

From Inside These Wild Ones is Book 3 in the Re-Membering Series.

EXCERPTS FROM UPCOMING BOOKS

From *An Ambitious Silence* (2025)

An Ambitious Silence

What it calls for is an elegant unraveling—
more accurate and stunning than ever before

sinking into an ambitious silence,
robust and cunning

Do something useful for a change—Listen
so deep and richly
the big ear wants to open through you,
remembering all.

Be unfashionable—
tear the ears off
the false notes.

Shake your feathers
and invite the fox and raven

Until oak reaches into you
and the deep waters gather.

Mud and Moon are your Elders.
You won't get far without them.

Chant Old Man Owl
and Sister Dawn unto you.

That ancient place within beckons.

Unfold it into your bones
and drum your skeletal fragments
until they dance.

Then, like a humble apprentice
pay the tuition for your truth

bartering for the next bold season
with the currency of your heart

letting an unreasonable love
claim you like a throne

and walk your blessed seduction home.

From *Becoming Beautiful Barbarians* (2025)

Off-Script

This is not a dress rehearsal.

This is an undress rehearsal—
We're undressing the stories we've rehearsed
for far too long.

This is not a blockbuster movie.

This is composter cinema—
The only heroes that will be rushing in
are the ones we see naked
in the morning mirror.

And that is more than enough.

With thistles and a raven's beak
we tear up the scripts we inherited.

They are what got us into the Big Trouble.

Liberation is leaking out
of every page of the book
we are writing.

There is no script worth a damn
that doesn't include
the voice of River

the cries of our ancestors
or the longings living in our bones.

For each mouthful of empty-calorie modernity,
we create a meal of new melodies.

For each megabyte of consumption,
we create a terabyte
of participatory dreaming.

With each breathe we forge
strange and novel toys
in service to the Grand Metabolism.

We are preparing a buffet of the future.

www.ingramcontent.com/pod-product-compliance
Lightning Source LLC
Chambersburg PA
CBHW071249070526
44583CB00017B/2385